A VIEW OF WATER

First published December 2005 by **shalom house poetry**, 31 The Cairn, Newtownabbey, County Antrim, BT36 6YF.

ISBN: 0 – 9551896 – 1 – 6
        978 – 0 – 9551896 – 1 - 6

Printed by Summit Printing
137 Gregg Street, Lisburn BT27 5AW
Tel: 028 9266 5038   Fax: 028 9266 1471
Email: info@summitprinting.co.uk

Layout of cover by Michelle Taylor and the original photograph taken by T. Honey.

This book has been funded through the support of the 'Awards for All' scheme.

A VIEW OF WATER

Tom Honey

Shalom
House
Poetry

Acknowledgments

The Shalom House poetry group gratefully acknowledges the 'Awards for All' scheme for its generous funding and support of this publication.

Thanks are also due to the Belfast Institute of Further and Higher Education (BIFHE) and the Shalom House Centre, Cliftonville Road, Belfast.

Tom gratefully acknowledges the help and encouragement given to him over the years by the following:-

The Scribblers' Group
The former Friday night group led by Carol Rumens
Dr Edith Newman Devlin
and, currently, his colleagues of the Shalom House Poetry group.

Some of the poems featured in this anthology have been previously published in *The Irish News, Fortnight, The Belfast Telegraph, The Dundalk Democrat, The Honest Ulsterman* (2003), *The Ulster Tatler, Omnibus* and *Bear in Mind*, an anthology concerning the Troubles issued in 2000. Poems also appeared in a number of publications produced by the New Belfast Creative Arts Initiative (NBCAI), including *The Lonely Poet's Guide to Belfast* (2003), *Ringing the Changes* (2004) and *BT1, The Poet's Code* (2005). A selection of Tom's poems also appears in *'Keeping The Colours New'*, an anthology of poems by Shalom House poetry group, published in 2003.

Tom Honey was born and brought up in Belfast, spending most of his life as a teacher in the city, except for a period of seven years in the sixties when he lived in Brazil. Because of his own interest in poetry he tried always to stimulate the children he taught towards an appreciation of writing and poetry. He then began writing poetry himself in the late seventies but it was only after retiring that he found more time for his own writing.

A poem of Tom's won joint first prize in a *Fortnight Magazine* competition sponsored by Greenpeace in 1987. In the Poetry Ireland / Cooperation North national poetry competition 1991, he won first prize with publication in a broadsheet on the theme, 'A Sense of Place'. As a consequence he received a scholarship to the then newly opened Poets' House in Portmuck, Islandmagee. In the 'Year of the Family' Writers' Awards competition in 1994 he also won first prize.

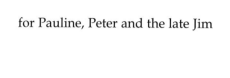

for Pauline, Peter and the late Jim

WAITING

In leaf-green light
where trees and water
share the shadows
a heron waits,
his bulky form
hunched as if
in summer somnolence.
It is a feigned lethargy
for the half-closed eyes
are vigilant
and, above the placid pond,
his pick-axe bill
is poised.

Contents

"the truant sky"

BLUEBELLS

We could have chosen better –
any of those blue-ceilinged mornings
May had brought, but now we climb
through overcast. Cave Hill frets
in a drizzle, glum as the pewter Lough.
I turn, responding to your cry.
Gathered in drifts beneath the trees
we find the truant sky.

HARVESTS

Finding the fissure in the skin
my thumbs press hard and split
the spiky husk wide open,
freeing the smile the chestnut keeps

concealed in its upholstered cot
for just this moment.
I smile too, as I must have done
through most of a life-time's autumns

for there is the pleasure of acquaintance
and the old delight in gathering
those red-brown pearls the windy nights
snatched from the trees for us. Cheesers

we called them, for conker was an import
like the comic-cuts we'd spend our penny on.
Fresh-firecoal chestnut-falls – the phrase
is Hopkin's and we recognise the glow.

Skewered and strung, we swung them in combat
till they shattered round our heedless heads.
Now, I work to redeem my youth, bury them
in labelled pots and pray them into growth.

COPPERPLATE

"Five minutes, lads, to warm your hands".
We'd thrust them in our pockets.
Classroom windows then were closed,
a ritual for writing time to ease
the chill his fresh-air fad imposed.
He'd challenge, "I want copperplate!"

Then set about instructing us
on height and width of letters,
demonstrated on a blackboard
lined in blue and red, prodding
us all insistently toward
the peak of his calligraphy.

Good writers had their work displayed
in merit order on a shelf.
Mine never made it there but stayed
among the undistinguished ones.
I laid a rather spiky strand
like barbed wire on the copybook.

What's more, I bore the legacy
for years until the day I watched
wavelets curling on a beach, loved
their rhythmic ease and tidy spill,
cut, at last, the classroom tentacle,
formed my own stroke, and use it still.

OLD LESSONS

The question put to us then
seemed academic –
what, in our view,
was Nature's greatest force?
With all the certainty of the uninformed
we fifteen-year-olds discussed the point,
veering from earthquakes and volcanoes
to wind in all its rages round the earth.
To his own query the teacher gave answer –
"Moving water."
Past his shoulder the window revealed
a lethargic sea nibbling at the strand.
Water? Debatable.

"Use your physics, lads.
Sixty two and a half pounds
in every cubic foot.
Think of the punch that's carried
in a wave!"

We hadn't thought. Were forced
to look at the phenomenon again.
Didn't know, decades back,
the Japanese had given it a name.

ENCOUNTERS WITH STEEL

A zing of stropped steel, then
my father brought the long blade
down across the virgin growth
about my lip and chin

I sat, eyes closed and cheeks
aquiver under lather while
the open razor zipped through
fuzz. It took no time at all.

Not so when I unsheathed
the cut-throat that first time
to shave myself, the handle,
mother of pearl, damp in my hand.

My unskilled shiftings through
a half an hour left blood darts
plentiful enough to shock
the pallid face the mirror showed.

A mild celebrity was mine
when I shaved beside my peers.
who put their trust in safety blades
but I stropped on for years.

The times demand the throwaway;
for family relics, no regret.
Stubbles now are brought to yield
to the best a man can get.

KID BROTHER

for Peter

Once, when you really were a kid,
I sent you, arms full of grubby books –
Livy, Virgil, Mathematics texts,
a Latin grammar, Shakespeare play –
to Harry Hall's in old Smithfield,
and promised a percentage of the gains.

An hour or so later a fusillade
of kicks shook the back door.
Piled on the step, Livy and Co.,
denied space even on Harry's floor.
Of you no sign. I'd like to think
I paid your portion anyway

but have my doubts. Yet many years on
I still lay task after task in your arms
and watch as each is competently met
and not a word of money changing hands.

RAISINS

Sardis behind us, its remaining columns
holding only sky, we came upon
the vineyards and our bus slowed again.
Baskets full of winking grapes were passed
from hand to hand to the road's edge.
There, on the flattened margins, spread
over sheets of plastic and cotton, lay
dismembered bunches, a highway
of bronzing fruit losing its freshness
to the sun. "Raisins," shouted everyone.
And all the way to Izmir we could see
a harvest shrivelling, another being made.

In a stone jar she used to keep them
stored, I remember, high on a shelf
and in a wordless ritual she'd place
a small heap on my desk when I ploughed
Latin furrows or climbed Higher Maths.
Sweets, in those days of rationing,
were absent friends. My books had grown
into a mountain unscalable for her
but she watched my slow ascent approvingly.
I didn't really want the raisins
but guessed she wanted me
to want them. My memory
is of munching through those study years
as if her store was inexhaustible.

BEGINNERS PLEASE NOTE

for T.P starting school

You have let August slip away
without a glance, your baby hours
discarded like a skin, your chatter
all about school. You flaunt your satchel
as proof of your new status. How could
you know that days will never be
the same. Under orders now
you will march daily to the clamour
of a bell. Time will follow your
shadow, pushing you on, however
well you run, however slow
you wish to go, and take a hand
in fattening that satchel. Year
by year its load will grow, wearying
your shoulder. But look on books
as batteries for a torch that will
bring light to the darkest places.
And it's your finger on the switch.
Yes, now it all begins – the big career,
so we'll indulge that first day tear.

STORY TIME

They smack lips noisily, a liberty
allowed, while I read to them
the tale of Charley Bucket as he
encounters with dazzled eyes
the unimaginable wonders
of the Chocolate Factory.
Twenty five small boys shadow him,
their hands with his on the Golden
Ticket, gluttony on their minds.
An orchestra of tongues leaps
to engage with endlessly suckable
gob-stoppers, gaily luminous lollies,
lickable wallpaper, a toffee apple tree.

Twenty five less one, his gaze
elsewhere, so unenraptured
by Dahl magic that I'm perplexed.
Later I hear the story
of that averted head and know
that no words of mine
could cheer him, nor any sweet
that Willie Wonka could design.

A LESSON LEARNED

Curtly I'd ordered him to stay behind
    then led the other children to the hall.
And stay he did, forgotten, while school dined.

Stayed, while I munched sandwiches and scanned
    the Times, and did my bit for staff-room craic.
Stayed, like Casabianca on the deck,

till, a half hour later I came back
    to find him staunching tears with jotter paper.
One small boy deprived of dinner.

I almost quailed before those brimming eyes,
    plied him with tissues and apologies,
wrapped some money in his sticky hand,

told him he'd make the shop if he ran.
    He'd set a marker in obedience,
and, misery over, took no offence.

LEAVE ME THE MEMORIES

for Margaret on her retirement

Year after year clouds gathered in my mind
when, weeks too early, shops would organise
their "Back to School" displays – sombre blazers,
pyramids of shoes and motley ties –
and I'd reproach myself for leisure thrown
away, lament the summer's wholeness gone, the days
adrift like petals prematurely blown,
and a new term's dull certainty.
That is, until this year. My sky is clear,
and summer now runs through September.
I locked a door in June; the new school year
will see another in the room I knew
so well, a voice replacing mine, new breath
to set aglow the embers. I can do
without such onerous privilege now. Leave
me the memories. I will indulge them
in the quiet hours, or when the seasons weave
nostalgia through my thoughts, recalling trails
where chestnuts lie or beeches rust through winter,
where in May the hawthorn spreads white veils
and lifts the mind to First Communion days.
I used to fill my arms with various fragrant
sprays and bring alive a classroom corner.
That door is closed I know, but you and I
believe the best is still before us and have
time in plenty to discover why.

TRENCH HOUSE REUNION

A stream of teachers fifty years long
was ending here. We, being the first,
knew our distinction so – the spring
gone dry, the house half derelict –
were we disposed to gather in the place
again, reunion mostly, but part wake ?
We were. A college photograph bore names
but matching these to faces beached by
careers now past would tax us all.

Every car rounding the curve of the drive
brought one more face to stimulate conjecture.
No country lads now in navy serge, V-necked
pullovers, shirt collars splayed like wings.
Fine suits, impressive ties, we looked
successful but smiled uncertainly,
edging towards each other, eyes picking
at the layered years. Faces came
like blurred reflections, then
the clarifying moment as names surfaced
and were seized.

Laughter, while tea was served, slapped
round the tables noisily. Old-remembered
stories were re-launched with ever greater
spread of sail. But in the backwash,
sober confidences too – dark words
like coronary, stroke, dementia.

Trench House gloomed in the background
as a last photograph was called.
Thirty two of us, some lecturers,
widened our smiles to shed the years
and camouflage the blemishes.
A month, a year away or maybe two,
the rumoured wrecking crew was gearing up,
soon to be heading our way.

"mouths gather stones"

WITNESS

Lights at the corner halt the bus
I travel on and I am briefly
neighbour to a group beyond
the window, men idling near a pub,
feet shifting restlessly, hands
pocketed, tones raucous though
the thrumming engine drowns their words.
A young man in his twenties, eyes lowered,
passes, edging round them near
the kerb. Flick-blade looks turn
on him. Mouths gather stones.
Though no one touches him
their swingeing laughter is an assault.
He draws so near me that I see
sweat on his brow, and a face
so wounded that it trails me
like a stifled moan long after
the bus has brought me home.

RAIDER

I sensed rather than saw
its swoop along the hedge,
heard the surge
in the sparrows' chittering.

But there - on my lawn! –
a sparrowhawk, talons locking
more tightly round its prize.
At my bedroom window

I sprang into rescue mode,
tapped sharply on the glass,
waved my arms wildly
like a flightless bird.

A yellow eye afforded me
a glance before the beak plunged,
scattering breast feathers
on the cowering grass.

I roared to reassert myself.
The hawk soared in mastery
and in the laurel's depths
a shudder lingered.

FLAGS IN SEASON

I

From their hibernation in dark corners,
wardrobes, chests of drawers, they waken
to the fever of July, and stretch
themselves in the loyal wind; they have a stake
in the proceedings and flex their colours
till they bulge like muscles, catch
the gleeful mood of impudent flutes
and jig to age-old tunes. They are
the showy guests in many a small street
and, mustered under the eaves at nightfall,
grow conspiratorial.

As children hurrying to school
we ran the gauntlet, nervously darting
under a lowering canopy of reds and blues.
House-top rowdies we thought them, certain
they brandished fists at our fleeing backs.
We too made fists but only in our pockets.
These days I can pass without sweaty palms
A row of boisterous Union Jacks.
It took time, but I no longer feel
them threatening. Seems better to relax.

II

Once I watched a flag die,
watched it slowly disintegrate,
tied to the crown of a larch
forgotten, its steady rate
of dissolution led by a wind
no longer loyal. Winter's purge
left a pale remnant shivering
on the staff. Spring's surge,
greening again the larch,
found the flag a feeble tongue,
all spirit gone, as March
left warp and woof undone,
till only threads clung, picked at
by birds with homes to run.
It seemed to me the boy I'd been
had seen a battle won.

IN MEMORY OF CYRIL MURRAY

Something of the darkness you'd lately
pulled yourself out from shadowed
your eyes that day, yet your wit,
still keen, punctured our best speeches.

Beneath our staff-room banter, though,
a sense of loss. Committed teacher
whom commitments drained, too late
we saw that we had not been

vigilant enough; now your retirement
and our rush of tributes, telling
you nothing you did not know
but never sought to advertise.

I phrased my wish for you in Irish,
I remember, to end my speech.
Go raibh blianta sona romhat –
may the years ahead be happy.

Just that; there were no intimations
that your future would be other
than we reckoned it. We pictured you
footloose in fragrant places around

Donegal, your easel in the heather,
your eye relishing the light
breaking through cloud round Errigal:
and you'd have music near, a tape

of Mozart maybe, delicate
in the mountain air –
unreal, unreal! All our goodwill
powerless to fend off terror,

your innocence no shield as killers
tore through your home one midnight,
mounted the stairs and found you
wide-eyed at your bedroom door.

FREEDOM OF THE STREETS

Scavenging in the early morning light
a fox has the school-yard to itself
before the scholars come.

In my own driveway a sparrow-hawk
begins to pluck
the stunned body of a dove.

They grow in confidence
the wild things, seizing the day
in our domain.

*   *   *   *

Heaped flowers mark where he died
the latest innocent who thought it safe
to walk home in the dark.

AFTERMATH

Sometimes the geese were heard, querulous
behind the six-foot fence, earning their
keep as quirky vigilantes while walky-talky
staccato broke out at intervals. Among
the trees, unsleeping eyes of cameras.
Police cars came and went. Doubts were
aired about security, so overnight
all changed. The judge and family,
many heavy crates, police, land-rovers
and the indifferent geese decamped
one dawn. Only a milkman observed.

The garden lay in a faint of apprehension.
Spoilers came, cautiously at first,
creeping in from the wings. Piece by piece
the lap-fence walked. Lead flashing,
wrested from the roof, went next and then
the harvesting of Bangor blues. The wind
pleasured itself among the naked joists.
Down came the house, precautionary act.
Then, hand-delivered, bagged, unbagged
litter took its place. At nightfall,
mattresses, settees, old T.V sets.

Dogs and mitchers shared the territory
by day; the nights grew raucous.
Big brother trees, assaulted, quietly
said their prayers; small shrubs took
what they got and winced, and yet each
year the cherry defied the degradation,
fired its salvo of blossoms in the air,
and year by year, kindling, undeterred,
in dark corners snowdrops and crocuses
gave notice that the calendar was theirs.

The garden quietly stirred.

FIVE FINGER STRAND

How you must have loved moments
like these on the strand, under
the high dunes and the cliffs,
the sun, gold turning bronze,
lowering into Trabreaga Bay.

I look for detail your painter's eye
would have delighted in, like how
the sand, combed into undulations
by the tide, catches the honeyed
light; how scattered wrack flares,
reveals its amber core, everything
made gentler at this hour –
sea holly on the upper shore,
the marram crowding the dunes.

I come in late homage, friend.
You could be walking just ahead
so strongly do I feel your presence,
but the sand remains untracked.

And all those images of Inishowen
redeemed for you the dark of Belfast,
your brush bringing them home.
Tears come, thinking of that final
image you beheld – the stranger
in a balaclava, gun in his hand.

THE CONNACHT

i.m. Conn and Audrey

That mastless hulk in a boatyard,
like a beached whale, bided your coming.
I imagine your heart rising to the lure,
your mind humming.

You wanted the sea's hubbub again
round that old prow, and wind enough
to slap new canvas into life;
yes, however tough

that job might be. It redefined you,
Conn, craftsman and sailor; your flair
never more surely applied.
Truly, a love affair.

Proud at the wheel of the hooker
they should have garlanded you
when first you sailed into Galway,
your craft made new.

　　　　　* * * * *

I remember that day of the wind,
a fretful, bullying one that threw
itself at children on their way home.
Did you fear it, Conn, as it blew

out of the southwest? Were those splendid
sails tormented till the waves took charge,
dooming Audrey and you
somewhere off Ards?

They took her body from the sea
that still holds yours. Are you at rest
in Connacht's cabin, easy
among the things you loved best ?

So many friendly homes now mourn
you, Conn, and miss you calling in,
remembering how you'd shout out
from the door – *have you the kettle on?*

STILLNESS OF SWANS

Below the trees the bank
was celebratory with crocuses.

The warm sun, a February surprise,
probed the sky's tumble of clouds.

Empty cans bobbed at the pond's corner
but it was too early for drinkers.

The wind drew a cool finger
across the water, rocking the swans.

Their ranked stillness drew my eye
towards the bank they faced.

A cluster of people, crouched, solicitous,
bent around a wounded swan.

One wing, underside up, lay across
its back. Among disordered feathers, blood.

"Happened last night, I suppose," said one
and sent our pained murmurs circling.

The swan formation, fixed on us,
seemed ceremonial in composure

And for a foolish moment I held still,
caught myself, head raised, listening.

A MORE THAN PASSING GLANCE

Today again the thin stream chokes
on garbage sticking in its throat.
The morning-after pond reviews
the beer cans tipsily afloat.
Beneath another night's tattoos
the footpath's tarmacadam smarts.
A downed election poster sulks
among the water-lilies' stars.

But look - here's something heartening;
the tufted vetch transfiguring
a stand of nettles, underrated flowers
released in blue and violet showers
that merit more than passing glance,
- a neon-bright exuberance.

PRAYER FOR CAVE HILL

In this whin-gold time of year,
make-over complete,
your forty greens enhanced
and all winged life
relishing your blessedness,
we know our good fortune
to live at your feet.
May you always be ever-renewable
ever viewable, ever big brother
to the city, *whatever the street.*

"pull the curtains wide"

SEEING

Yesterday April
pulled the curtains wide
showed me a gilded pond
of shaken chain-mail
a stream like javelins in flight
a blazon of whins on Squire's Hill
and through the grass a host
of dandelions daring to beguile.

I stared, astonished, seeing
the utterly familiar
so utterly beautiful.

EDITH

I have a photo of her set aside,
one taken while she, settled on a chair,
     listens, attentive, to a boring guide
one summer in a Lithuanian park.
     No other in the group accompanying her
attends much to him, as their eyes
     wander to other features here and there.
And so, again, in other strange locations
     couriers discover how she listens well,
enjoy her rapt look and her patience,
     absorbed, it seems, by what they have to tell.

And then her questions follow and we all
     learn to put questions for ourselves.
But how could it be otherwise for one
     like her, so given to the quest for truth
and knowledge, quizzing others and herself,
     leading us through the world's great books.
And so it's little wonder how she draws us,
     students one and all, each week.
Three hundred plus, maturer specimens,
     they come, however wintery the street.

THE FEBRUARY THRUSH

I pick my steps on icy pavements
and grumble at the morning's greyness.
Somewhere ahead a thrush declares its presence
with a rush of notes. Through a watery eye
I search a leafless chestnut till I see him,
a blur on the crown's tip against the sky.

    Hi there hi
    why hurry by
                see me see me
                I sit on the tip
                                my tree my sky
                                stay a while
                I fling I fling
                my singing silver
free free
that's my style

I stay, revelling in his bright shower,
longing for a tune to gleam with his
in gladdening this February hour.

LIME TREES

It stays in memory as a cameo –
the veiled head, the coif a white reef
islanding her face, her voice low
as she read to us something improving
but too spiritual for that warm June morning,
the pious thermals drifting away from us.

There were, I remember, lime trees
immersed in sunlight, a green lucency
that charmed me into reverie
so that I heard nothing more
until a blackbird, hidden cantor,
broke in with his own *laudate*.

But nothing of the text read then
remains with me. Yet even now the sight
of limes lit by the ascending sun –
haloed leaves grown luminous –
stirs in me unfailingly
a sense of the numinous.

VENTURING

for Janice and Jimmy

It seems strange to follow you both
into the mild surf for the sole reason
that I want to learn to paint.
Our ankles refract in water that scarcely
deepens however far we advance.
Your brush piles sky and water,
rock and wrack on the page,
the sea's menace flowing from the swirling
tip even on a day as calm as this.
Compared to you she moves hers
like a subtle dancer, everything
lighter, veined with mystery.
her washes delight me, but
whose brush do I follow?
I have set page after wasted page
drifting off on the quiet current,
watching on each a snake of water
make free with my paintwork.
I trusted your word about the tide
still companionable about us,
but why, along the sky's full rim,
is there nowhere a hint of land?

SOLO RUN

It happens every winter;
happened last week: the sun,
like a kid grounded for misdemeanours
sulked for days behind the overcast,
till, snatching the chance of an open window,
bounded down through bundled cloud
to stretch his legs on the hills.
The fields smiled to see him
and the jubilant trees watched agog
as he cartwheeled around the woods
and headed off for a dip in the lough.
He was soon cornered again, of course,
but not before billing future attractions,
the arrival of summer's big-top.

DIFFERENT STRANDS

for Pauline

An immigrant vocabulary
has come and occupies our house,
a needle-worker's litany
that baffles me, yet I admit
to savouring the euphony
of names I hear, like double treble
herring bone, bullion stitch, feathering
French knots, picots, seeding, couching
Trapunto, stumpwork embroidery.

Needle in hand she sits by the lamp,
silken skeins unravelling at her feet
like shredded rainbow. What plan
has she in mind this time?
I'll be invited to pass judgement,
my ignorance no bar and I'll incline
to admiration; those stranger-words
have now won residency, and foster
beauty in the space they occupy.

SHINING ARMOUR

The compliment – for I sensed no guile –
turned my head a little.
"Thomas," she said and her smile,
resting on me like an accolade,
redeemed the cliché. "You're a knight
in shining armour!" So she repaid
the lift that saved her from a long walk
in a downpour. Rain spears broke
against the windshield. Our talk
was of poetry and her next reading.

For days afterwards her compliment
nourished my thoughts, breeding
the sweetest notions of self-esteem.
I confess I liked the pose of knight,
finding a new gloss in an old dream.
Chivalry called, and oh the ache
to be seen as valorous!
Dragons or windmills I could take
or leave, but there was a deal more
out there needing the lance.

In steadier moments, alas, I knew the score.
Knightliness was out. Only the suit
of armour was mine. Who but me
had fashioned its parts from boot
to helmet. I'd clanked day after day
to school in it, wore my Sunday best
in it, let my voice go astray
in the depths of it. What chance now
to free myself of this carapace,
hear the real me, see the real face?

THE CAMARGUE

"A hundred snowy horses unconfined -
racing, spray-curled, like waves before the wind"
       'Horses on the Camargue', Roy Campbell

Our bus slows for the photo shot
but nobody alights, or tries
for pictures through streaked windows.

Anyway, the horses, mottled – white
all five of them, stand bunched to face
the slanting rain, heads drooped

Damp manes and tails inert
like engines stalled in the drowned field,
their fire inconsiderately doused.

And black bulls - promised too –
are pointed out behind
low hedges, scarcely in view

A pink drizzle of flamingos,
are poised like stamps in an album.
The bus swishes on.

Somewhere between tour guide and poet
my expectations sink
in soggy ground.

MARKET DAY IN LES VENS

Yes, there was plenty on the stalls
that lined the medieval streets,
piled loaves and cheeses, clustered grapes,
pears, fish, fowl, wines and artefacts
of olive wood and bright ceramics –
all cheerily photographic.
Instead, I turned my camera downwards,
to scan the ground, waiting to snap
the clean, flagged spaces under
every stall, the polished cobbles
in between. No sign of fish heads,
rotten fruit, cheese rinds or empty cans,
no drifts of crisp bags, stubbed cigarettes.
Nothing for sweepers' brooms.
Streets fresh as the glaciers we'd seen
glistening above Chamonix.
If I were set to write a brochure
for the place, I'd praise its spotlessness,
sing less of chateaux and the vines.

PRIORITIES

Around these parts we keep our dogs
and hedges on a lead; summer hears
mower answer mower across modest
lawns, sees the exuberance
of privet civilly contained.
And so, the vacant house behind mine
posed a threat; its garden's rampant
growth undid my peace.

The privet startled with its vigour,
shadow-boxing when the air breathed.
Turbulent in gusts, it rioted
the length of my overlap fence,
a lout glooming over my standards,
mocking my barbered shrubs.
Then in July its image altered;
the privet creamed with blossom.

I watched the butterflies arriving
one late afternoon, small tortoiseshell
in gentle competition for the privet flower.
I tried a count, but their restiveness
made it impossible.
See-sawing wings
set embers glowing and the fire
transformed the privet's commonness.

But before summer's end windows
no longer vacant frothed with muslin.
An energetic couple brought house
and garden back to the tailored norm.
The privet, felled in a hail of woodchips,
shrank beside my fence like a whipped dog.
They built a patio and there at weekends
on recliners milk the season's fitful sun.

BREAKDOWN

No hand in years has tried to curb
the privet hedge now shouldering
her front door like a drunk, scuffing
the paintwork ceaselessly on windy days.
It bulges out to halve the pavement's width
yet there are no complaints. Neighbours
armed with shears once offered help
but were rejected, so they stay away.
Her old red Ford squats in the drive
on perishing tyres. Years back
her man's new Audi sat there
but it went when he went. Scarcely
noted now her quiet comings
and goings through the back door.
There waist-high grasses sigh
beneath a swing's dark rusted spar.

Children mutter *Witch's House*
as they dash by in the dark.

NEIGHBOUR

They shared a hedge, neighbours
who never chanced a conversation.
Words, she told herself, would
lose themselves in the privet's bulk.
So she clipped her side discreetly
and pictured his actions by the sounds
he made as trowel clinked, or shears
snipped, accompanying his wheezy breath.

Sometimes, when streaming sunlight
drenched the hedge, she saw his stooping
form, an incomplete mosaic; white tufts
of hair, bent shoulders vague as through
a beaded curtain. Older than her, she
guessed though she couldn't see his face.
A hedge apart, a quarter mile by road,
they tended their gardens and their thoughts.

Once, as she planted autumn bulbs,
a rough cough, feet away, startled her
and its harsh repetition followed
his slow circuit of the garden.
She could have muttered something
but let her sympathy subside, unspoken.
Days of untidy silence spoke his absence,
then days stretched into weeks.

Winter stripped the mountain ash, disclosed
his upstairs window framed in branches.
Panes, uncurtained, lacked a woman's hand
and the only hand she saw at the blind
seemed frail as a leaf. Sometimes,
when sleep was slow to come, she'd see
his window lighted, a buoy in a sea
of heaving boughs.

At times she heard – or thought she heard –
a faint far cough. The day the blind
stayed drawn she lingered near the hedge
but heard only the sound of her own breathing.
She pictured his garden in retreat, sensed
the sting of things neglected and chances lost.
Then came the sound of car doors slamming,
the shuffle of feet, hushed voices.

She turned from the hedge sighing, breath
whitening in the frosty air, her body cold.

THE LARCH

Dominates a neighbour's garden
its longest branch fanning the air
round his indifferent gable, while
he and his windows look elsewhere.

Even in winter nudity it keeps
its benedictory pose, serene,
Francis-like, welcoming neighbourhood birds,
– songsters, raptors and all between.

It was their terraced stage. Starlings,
like clustered fruit, would hog the high
crown, all whistles, clicks and squeaky shoe
sounds, till they exploded into flight.

The hooded crow also visited,
burdening a high bough, grey head
swivelling and buccaneer eye
raking the branches' leafy spread.

Solo performers had their own air-time
- thrush, blackbird, robin- and I found
myself happily searching the boughs
for silhouettes that matched the sounds.

A year now and no song among the leaves.
Have they found more lavish givers,
sites where they forage unafraid,
mixtures to lure the sweetest singers?

Yes, I miss the larch's visitors,
the bird song, evenings, when I dined;
miss, too, those sharp eyes watching,
mornings, when I raise the blind.

"the voice I listen for"

SURVIVOR

It must have been a near thing
with a cat that left his wings
askew, and hanging so they seem
like blackbird hand-me-downs, the sheen
gone from the plumage. Survivor
now from seasons past, familiar
on my lawn, his unkempt look
wins favours, though starlings loot
the bread I throw. That said, he knows
how to sell himself, for I note
at evening, time and again,
on that larch bough at my garden's end
his ragged silhouette appears
and, well before stars emerge, he stars.
Hedgerows ring with a backing choir
but it's his voice that I listen for.

NOTES FROM THE PAST

Dad's soprano resonated through family lore
so constantly I often tried to picture him
aged twelve in old St. Joseph's church before
the altar singing Adeste at Christmas Mass.

"Crowds came to hear him," aunts used to say,
their pride in recollection ignoring
the piety of those who came to pray,
buoyed by the joy of nativity.

The story had its villain too – the choirmaster.
"Kept him singing far too long. Should have left
the voice to rest before it broke. A disaster,"
thought the aunts, seeing a talent squandered.

Once, for the four of us, from his old repertoire
Dad mined a hymn about a Green Hill Far Away
and took off in a strained falsetto, to restore,
I suppose, a remembered solo glory.

I was the eldest and it pains me still
that my unmanageable sniggers set the others off.
It was like targeting a bird, watching it fall
at our feet. Dad stopped mid-note. He didn't scold.

Just said, half-theatrically, half in pain,
"I'll never sing again." Mind you, he did,
but we knew that day we'd heard his requiem
for what was long beyond recovery.

A LETTER FROM BELFAST

Father's scribbles covered old envelopes,
newspaper margins, dockets; a pleasant
rounded hand, its decorative confidence
something that we never matched, lacking
his stylish sense. He relished using capitals,
fashioning outlines to meet his whims.

One such, his A in upper case, I liked.
Its tent profile he scrapped, devised instead
an arching shape that looked almost like a symbol
in a tourist guide. Through half-closed lids
I'd see it as a tiny caravan, a covered wagon
that strayed outside the alphabet.

And I believed that solid man, my da, hid
a romantic strain. That dreamy eye, matching
the blue drift of his pipe smoke, led me
to wonder where he might be journeying.
Belfast, a place of meagre expectations then,
had cramped his hopes, but yet he never left.

Abroad for him was Glasgow, five lean years
Apprenticeship. No package holidays,
no foreign parts, he seemed content to hear
of them through us. He's dead these forty years
yet I still use his A in upper case
when writing off to places he'd have loved –
to CANADA, the U.S.A, to RUSSIA and BRASIL.

FLOWERS

Though we were children then, we noticed
how her face brightened in the park
beside the flower beds, her eye
gathering their brilliant images
set in concentric rings of butter yellow,
rust, vermilion; and the scents!
She carried home the memory to our small
street, a desert of grey pavement.

But now she wanders through a garden
of our own where she is circled round
with blooms and we, despairing, watch
her snatching at their heads,
uprooting newly planted things;
our pain is not the loss of flowers.

REFLECTION

The mirror gave you back your tired smile.
We watched the nodded greeting as your words
came haltingly. The moving lips you saw
were reassuring so you talked some more.
We should have interrupted yet we kept
our distance, troubled by this new decline.
"I've asked her in for tea," you murmured then,
"Why won't she come?" We could not bear
your eyes' bewilderment but took your arm
and led you slowly to the open air
to listen to a blackbird somewhere near.
We covered every mirror from then on
but found no cover for our growing fear.

ADRIFT

Had we let you go
Out the door in slippers,
Handbag corpulent with all
Your magpie gleanings,

Where would that crippled compass
Have led you, seeking home
At the far end
Of a generation?

Who would pilot you back
Your smiles adrift
On the straits between
You and strangers,

Your urgency stalled
At some kerb
By the speeding wheels?
Find haven here

The safe side of the door.
That mute-tongued lock you sigh
So often over signs love;
So did the gate you used

To block the stairs from us.
This mothering we learned
From you, and so much else.
We travelled on your breath

Till time filled all our sails.
But now you drift in strange
Seaways, the mind's Sargasso.
Know that in the mist we hover;

Ride easily in our lee.

BACOPA

A full year it has flowered,
strung between May and May,
hoisting through the dark months
its tiny blooms and they
like flakes snatched from the snow.
But now this morning signs
of rust among the green, a slow
dilution of its bridal shine.
Has it outrun its strength, unlikely
now to see the summer through?
Its tiring blossoms show
winter has jumped the queue.
Better allow it space
to die; accept its year of grace.

HOSPITAL NIGHTS

Nine floors up we are as far removed
from traffic noise as from tobacco smoke.
Deepening hammocks of shadow
draw the ward towards sleep
but I sense a quiet wakefulness
in the still forms on other beds.

Signatures gathered hours before
commit our bodies to procedures
we have had briskly explained.
"Straight-forward, really, though
there is an element of risk. You may
experience some discomfort..."

Above each bed a sign reminds
the morning trolley lady to guide
her teetering tea-cups past us.
Murmurs creep in from the corridor;
nurses gossiping, night voices
too indistinct to trouble us.

From a dark corner, falteringly,
an old Fermanagh farmer frets
about the price of lambs. Uneasily
I drift into his fevered stream
and find the dark hours troubled
with low bleatings from the fields.

A SONG DEFERRED

On the pyracantha by the fence
flame berries still glisten
though a blackbird pair
have cleaned the upper boughs.
Cock and hen take turn about
to gorge. They know the harvest
and the time for choicest picking.
Know themselves hawk-free, cat-free
inside the armoured bush, and so,
methodically, unhurriedly, steadily
they work their way downward,
eating only what they need.
It's hoped when all the fruit is gone
they'll pay a dividend of song.

LIFT-OFF

On a raised path they travel
cresting the grassy slope,
not far above eye-level,
power-walkers, strollers,
dogs, a jogging pair,
all cloud companioned,
all unaware
how the favouring sky
lends them distinction.
There seems no reason why
they couldn't take flight,
enter another element.

I too have been there
content just taking the air.
Yet, time and again,
when I view that peopled sky
I feel I'm missing something
driving by.

A WALK IN THE RAIN

a goose herds its family
out of our path

the may is confetti now
on the wet grass

pools in commotion
gather the sky

a man with a fishing rod
tends to the fly

clouds of cow parsley
shimmer with flower

relaxed in the downpour
a blackbird sounds the hour

"eavesdropping on wear and tear"

TINNITUS

Less a ringing than a low sibilance,
a slow puncture in the head, a sound
I've almost come to terms with, excepting
times like now when, trying out thoughts
in lines across a page, I resign myself
to this misted silence. If, in the noisy
flotsam of the day it seems withdrawn,
I need only settle down to think
or play at shaping verse to bring it
like a wreath of midges round my head
until I feel I'm eavesdropping on wear
and tear. Though there are mornings when
I seem to drown in torrents, mostly
day opens as it ends, in a long-drawn
sigh like fine sand falling and I pretend
indifference to the hour-glass in my head
endlessly spilling irrecoverable grains.

REMEMBERING

I had no problem in my younger days
when memory was a vast but friendly hall
that gave shelf space to anything at all –
phone numbers, music, names, a telling phrase,
stars, flowers, fashion, the football craze,
titles and authors in the Booker trawl,
the latest poems on art's gable wall
– a store of wonders in a wondrous maze.

But much there nowadays is veiled in dust,
and stacked untidily in growing piles,
so far accessible - but only just,
for there's a deal of clutter in the aisles;
and there I rummage with uncertain sight
for fragments of what once had brought delight.

BOVRIL MAN

To take to sea wearing only pyjamas,
his legs and arms encircling
the neck of a giant Bovril jar
seemed to my boyish eyes
like bravado gone too far.
But he looked happy in his striped attire
smiling, giving the odd wave
in spite of grey-green rollers
threatening a watery grave. . .
That mammoth long-ago poster
caused my craven heart to quaver;
explains why I never took to Bovril
quite sure that tea was safer.

BLITZ MEMORY

The all-clear brought us dashing
from our homes to join school-mates
gorging on stories of land mines,
whistling bombs and death.
The stench of burning was all around
and the indiscriminate crack-crack
in the fires' heat. Flames, bright
sailing sparks fed the red sky.
We skipped over gushing mains water,
slithered on shattered slates, dodged
the downed telegraph wires,
all of us racing to view the mill
that had choked life out of Sussex Street.
Suddenly, in a doorway,
a soot-grimed Cassandra appeared –

"Yiz all wanted them, didn't yiz?
well, now yiv got them!"

she bawled to the Gerry-lovers
of the city, turned from us,
slammed the door, sending the last
of her panes into the street.

COUNTRYMAN

No matter that he has been fifty years
away from cattle, barns, potato drills,
the cut of countryman, confirmed by a face
that maps the weathering of earlier times,
has never left him. City dweller, yes,
but not a city man. Look at him now,
perched on that bollard near the kerb
shaken by traffic on the Antrim Road,
his pipe a seal on his contentedness
as if he'd spent the morning at the hay.

And that's how I remember Patrick
in far-off summers – he and his brothers,
brows streaming, pitchforks glinting,
and the stacks multiplying
in the stubbled field.

I touch the car horn, wave; he tilts
his stick. At once I see those clean-cut
acres, catch the fragrance still.

NAN KANE

"Flowers keep her young",
they said, as sills glowed
with bonny jeans, geraniums.
Spring was always in her mind
through every winter.
Trees she loved, the neighbour's
Yew excepted. Bulky, sombre,
it cut her field of visions
but she missed little, anyway
and in the lengthening summer
could watch the street all day.
Family called constantly,
pleased to meet her wants.
But last year, reprovingly,
said the house looked fine,
didn't need painting. Any number
of homes around looked worse.
Unspoken was the wonder
that someone of her years
would want the painters in.
But ladders soon appeared
and the job was done.
No day without a change
of wardrobe and a hint
of colour on the lips.
Hair faultless, elusive scent,
earrings matching her pastel shades
she bloomed among blooms.
The window was her carriage
to the world. She could presume
upon the goodwill of the street,
her smile, her wave almost queenly.

Glossy magazines delighted her.
"White," she'd say serenely
to visitors, "is in this year".
A week ago spring slipped
back to winter mode. On oxygen
in hospital she quipped
that the mask had upset her hair.
But Nan, just short of ninety-nine
had no more time to spare.

WEEKEND COTTAGE

i.m. Jim

Mildewed walls, sour sting of soot,
a range rust-blistered. In the grate
a jackdaw's scaffolding of twigs.
Little for us to celebrate.

But we gave our borrowed cottage
months of weekends; brought back the colour
to its cheeks; saw to the chimney's throat,
helped the sun heal the dank corners.

Jim painted on the staircase wall
the Seven Dwarfs in bright ascent.
The children took to them and made
Hi ho, hi ho, their bedtime chant.

Mornings saw them in fragrant fields
chasing the baler on its round.
Straw-pricked arms and skin aglow
charted their days lived far from town.

Lamplight; then a rush of stories,
patchy chronicles per child.
Plans were sleepily considered.
The dwarfs heard everything and smiled.

But winter's talons stripped the gold
of summer. Damp rooms, choked flue,
a privy comfortless and chill
undid us. Disenchantment grew.

The weekends died and jackdaws claimed
the smokeless chimney. Cobwebbed panes
told much. Once, after thieves had been,
I visited the derelict again.

Sad shell! But there by the staircase
the dwarfs still climb with undimmed cheer,
expectant faces seeking Snow White –
Gone. Gone many a long year.

A SENIOR'S VILLANELLE

The years lie heavy on my shoulders now
and yet I feel I still have much to do
I'm mobile only as my bones allow.

I should take living like the quiet cow
refining matters with a patient chew
The years lie heavy on my shoulders now.

Yet here I am still following the plough
hopeful of reaping what in time falls due.
I'm mobile only as my bones allow.

A fruitful harvest bends the apple bough
gives promise of a stimulating brew
The years lie heavy on my shoulders now

Give me a potion that will clear my brow
help me consider everything anew
I'm mobile only as my bones allow.

I still have visions though I wonder how,
gained I suppose, from people such as you
The years lie heavy on my shoulders now
I'm mobile only as my bones allow.

THE WATERWORKS, BELFAST

Memories of boyhood spent within
its modest acres gladden me still.
All its explorable joys, fullest
in summer, ours for one shilling a year.
We tortured every hanging bough;
wrestled in happy heaps until
we ran with sweat; cooled again
with feet in the moss-lapped stream,
then, jam-jars in hand, menaced
the fleeing spricks. Only a blast
of the ranger's whistle sobered us.
A bell at dusk would gather our
dishevelled band and set us running
before the gates were closed, for bye-laws,
yes, weighed somewhat more than now.
The bell is long gone and the bell-post
levelled, and gates no longer signify.
No ranger with a whistle, but instead
a man with a long pole fishing tinkling
beer cans from the water. He gathers
bottles from the bushes and builds them
in a pyramid, brown, white and green,
on a wheel-barrow. Cans packed in bags
hang from the handles. When he moves
the stale smell follows in his wake.
If there were walls they'd ache
with slogans; instead, the tarmac path
is made to carry tribal taunts.

Still, I take my Sunday stroll here.
On sharp winter days I've squinted
at the sun's brilliant disc, dazzled
by the decanted radiance
across the ice: saw with relief
spring's catkins soften the nakedness
of willows hunkered by the edge.

How easy on silky summer mornings
to forget the city pressing round;
to share the closeness of the hills
and see the gulls and wild fowl
as detail on a painted pond.
And Cave Hill, tawny in autumn,
like an old circus lion wearied
by too many tricks, lounging
in sleepy vigilance above us.

Two years ago machines moved
into action; thrusting, gouging,
they redefined the bank, heaping
rubble till islets formed off-shore.
Now in their tiny sanctuary the ducks
and swans build for the future.
I saw last spring seven cygnets
take to the water, so closely
following the swan they seemed
magnetised, the V of each wake
merging as they piped their hellos
to the world. And there have always
been swans here. Swans and these waters
kindled in early childhood this lingering
fondness, this confidence that what is here
has settled into permanence.

"still a stretch to go"

THE JOURNEY

My garden hasn't much to show
this Christmas day – just those
three yellow roses, feigning gold
where the wan sun touches them
but fails to break the cold.
Sprung from one stem they ride
like three crowned heads, and sway
wind-stirred and purposeful
as though travelling a way
that's hazardous this time of year.
They're through the winter solstice
but they've still a stretch to go.
Now the sun deserts them
and the sky is full of snow.

CONVERSION

For all the clustering whiteness
of his hair and meditative pose
in church last week Cloot Connery
was agent of my boyhood woes
when my ripe imagination saw him
as a kind of Dane. What terror
when he swept with guldering band
of yobs towards us, souring our summer,
their bin-lids and brush shafts
making thunder in our street. We ran,
our gang preferring any other day
for battle, choosing to defy them
from behind closed doors.
So tough was Cloot my timorous eye
saw muscles in the undulations
of his hair. Height and the loudest voice
confirmed for me his fearsomeness.
But time gives reason to rejoice.
I scanned that pious figure, so still,
monk-like in the long coat he wore,
and came to recognise that Cloot
had torched his long-boat years before.

GEORDIE

The topknot on a shaven head,
grave young face above a flare of saffron,
sandaled feet,
left me agape that day in Royal Avenue
all those years ago.
He was an exclamation in the street,
I, the question mark that tailed him.

Clearly a monk.
Lama, maybe, from some monastery
above the tree-line, close
to the rafters of the world.
I almost sensed dark rooms
resonant with chant; incense clouds,
butter-lamps in holy places.

But - why was he here?

A small man in overalls stopped him.

"Geordie, oul mate, wha' 'bout ya?"

Smiles. A handshake.

"I'm awright, Sam. 'Bout yerself?

Tibet dissolved in the colloquial exchange.
I'd seen my first of Hare Krishna folk.

Often they'd bloom like suddenly opening
marigolds among Cornmarket crowds,
all tinkling music, cheerful chant
and I'd speculate that Geordie
was the tall one with the tambourine.

They've all gone from our streets, so
where is he now? Plump and middle-aged
behind a bar, or coursing the town
in his own black taxi ?

I rather hope he's still in saffron
somewhere, fingering beads, taking
his own meditative measure of the world.

THE FALLS OF IGUAÇU

No photograph, no film,
nor the plane's accommodating circuit
        to whet appetites
prepared us to be stunned;
        to absorb
perpetual thunder in the humid air,
        to be dazzled
by the toppling brilliance of the cataracts,
        their endlessly twisting manes
of violent water so mesmeric
        that to move from point
to viewing point was
        always a wrench.

        Impossible
to try a count but our guide-book
        claimed to know –
two hundred and seventy falls
        taking the plunge
on the Iguaçu.
        Their leap
from the cliffs' vast basalt lip
        raised hundred metre
        towers of spray,
bridging the gorge's monstrous throat
        with a jumble of rainbows.

        My camera
and my postcard of superlatives. . .
        made poor work of
                the spectacle

I have only this reel in my head
        to rely on.

VISITING SKELLIG MICHAEL

Leaving the shelter of Bolus Head
our small craft bucked in the Atlantic heave.
The Kerry coast dipped and rose.

My back to the tiny cabin, I stared
uneasily at the whirling serpent of our wake
chasing our too low stern.

Spray laced the air, white-chipped water
raced around us. It gave little comfort knowing
that, ages before, ox-hide currachs

had coursed these seas for centuries.
We-tourists or pilgrims-kept our own thoughts.
Ninety minutes passed before we circled

Little Skellig, dung-whitened,
held in a restless net
of fulmars, gannets and guillemots.

Skellig Michael fronting us seemed
so precipitous the wonder was
that anyone could find a footing.

A French couple again kissing as if
they had a quota to fulfil before landfall
on that rock still redolent of saints.

An ocean crag, it took what all
the wildest storms could hurl
yet cradled those frail men

who wove their lives in prayer,
curbed appetites and spent their hours,
their years relishing their heritage.

Six hundred steps cut into rock
led upwards. Exhilarated by the wind
we climbed steadily,

then moved towards the huts,
small cells of corballed stone
where the extraordinary was done.

Under the low roof
the great turmoil of wind
and water sank

Till in that holy space
it sounded like the murmur
of old litanies.

Amazement silenced us
but, on the sea again,
prompted our Deo Gratias.

TENT

After reading 'Awareness', by A. de Mello

On my chosen site poles are set
pegs driven into firm ground
the canvas pulled taut.

Security, even Spartan comfort;
the excluded sky a mystery
put aside. Respite of a sort.

But a wind rises, throwing
torrents against the tent
and damp is showing.

The canvas throbs in growing gusts.
I sag like the guy-ropes,
the slackening posts,

till the wind's unflagging might
dismantles everything
leaves me to the night.

UNEXPECTEDLY

My morning takes a jolt encountering
the saplings – two weeks planted in the park –
now broken-backed, their branches
straining down like anguished arms.
Night hid the hands that shattered them,
each slender trunk snapped on its stake,
its pallid fibres gaping at the sun,
sap rising now to no good purpose.

I rail at such delinquent ways
and walk to clear my suffocation,
making for the hill's crest
to gain a view of water.

How the pond leaps frenziedly,
its surface prodded into dancing
by a swaggering wind bent
on its own choreography.

Suddenly a dozen swans
lift up in unison their wings,
a rise and fall mimicking
the peaks and hollows of the waves.

A startling synchronicity,
a ballet, spontaneous, ephemeral.
Of course it should have been to music
but I am happy just to sing.